D0603775

For Dorothy – J.B.

In loving memory of Mary McIntosh McDiarmid – J.D.

Let There Be Peace copyright © Frances Lincoln Limited 2009
Text copyright © The Reverend Jeremy Brooks 2009
Illustrations copyright © Jude Daly 2009
Title lettering by Sally Swart

First published in Great Britain and the USA in 2009 by
Frances Lincoln Children's Books, 4 Torriano Mews,
Torriano Avenue, London NW5 2RZ
www.franceslincoln.com

Acknowledgements
Page 11, top left: Vardit Fertouk, aged 8, reproduced by permission of Duncan Baird Publishers;
top right: © *Hear Our Prayer Everywhere*, 1790 S Hickey Road, Morgantown, IN 46160, USA. Pages 12-13: first published in
Bridge of Stars, reproduced by permission of Duncan Baird Publishers, London/Thorsons, New York.
Page 26: David Adam, from *The Edge of Glory: Prayers in the Celtic Tradition,* Triangle Publishing, by permission of SPCK.
Pages 28-29: Sy Miller and Jill Jackson ©1955 renewed 1983 by Jan-Lee Music (used by kind permission).
The publishers apologise to any copyright holders they were unable to trace and would like to hear from them.

British Library Cataloguing in Publication Data available on request

ISBN: 978-1-84507-530-9

Illustrated with acrylics
Set in Usherwood Book

Printed in China
1 3 5 7 9 8 6 4 2

Let There Be Peace

Prayers from Around the World

Selected by the Reverend Jeremy Brooks

Illustrated by Jude Daly

F

FRANCES LINCOLN
CHILDREN'S BOOKS

Praying for Peace

All over the world, people pray to God for peace. And all over the world people are fighting wars – and sometimes it seems to be the same people who pray for peace and then fight the wars.

Each religion is different, and sometimes people fight because they think their religion is right and others are wrong. But I hope this book of prayers will show that in many ways different religions have a great deal in common. And when we see that we share many beliefs with other faiths, it is harder to fight them over the things where we are different.

So why should we pray for peace? When we pray, we speak to God, but we also speak to ourselves. The last prayer in this book says, 'Let there be peace on Earth, and let it begin with me.' If we remember that peace begins with us, and if we act in peaceful, not aggressive ways, then it will begin with us.

As you read the prayers from around the world, remember that people of all ages from every country have also wanted peace. So we need not fear that people from other countries are the ones who want to start war: we all pray for peace.

My prayer for you all is that these prayers will help you to pray for peace in a a world at war, and that peace will begin in each of our hearts.

If there is to be peace in the world,
There must be peace in the nations.

If there is to be peace in the nations,
There must be peace in the cities.

If there is to be peace in the cities,
There must be peace between neighbours.

If there is to be peace between neighbours,
There must be peace in the home.

If there is to be peace in the home,
There must be peace in the heart.

Written over 2,500 years ago
by Lao-Tzu, founder of Taoism,
China

The following prayers were written by people living in countries
at war. In Northern Ireland, Protestant and Catholic Christians
have fought each other. In Bosnia, Christians and Muslims
have been enemies. In the Middle East, Christians, Jews
and Muslims have all been at war.

When tomorrow I open my eyes
I should like to hear the news
all the children in the world
are waiting for:
that peace, the Redeemer, has come.

Written by Vardit Fertouk, aged 8

Jesus,
love me, protect me
and give me a place of peace to grow into.
Amen.

Written by an 8-year-old child,
Northern Ireland

O God, you are peace.
From you comes peace,
To you returns peace.
Revive us with a salutation of peace
And lead us to your abode of peace.

Muslim daily prayer

In this city, where gunshots are almost as common as handshakes,
let us pray that two enemies will shake hands.
That makes four hands at peace with each other.

In this city, where woundings outnumber healings,
let us pray that the numbers do somersaults.

Written during the 1990s conflict,
Bosnia

From the hearts of peaceful souls
may a flag of peace unfurl
to fall from the sky
like a vast parachute
on to a region of war.

May enmities flounder,
tiring themselves
to exhaustion beneath the parachute of peace.

Written during the 1990s conflict,
Bosnia

*Living in peace does not just mean that we do not fight against
other people. We also need to live in peace with our world
and look after it properly. The following prayers remind us to do this.*

The world was not left to us by our parents.

It was lent to us by our children.

Traditional prayer,
Africa

All ye under Heaven! Regard Heaven as your father,

Earth as your mother

and all things as your brothers and sisters.

Shinto prayer,
Japan

Creator, open our hearts

to peace and healing between all people.

Creator, open our hearts

to provide and protect for all children of the Earth.

Creator, open our hearts

to respect for the Earth, and all the gifts of the Earth.

Creator, open our hearts

to end division, violence, and fear among all.

Thank you for the gifts of this day and every day.

Native American prayer written by Alycia Longriver

May there be peace in the higher regions; may there be peace in the firmament;

May there be peace on Earth. May the waters flow peacefully;

May the herbs and plants grow peacefully;

May all the divine powers bring unto us peace.

The supreme Lord is peace. May we all be in peace, peace, and only peace;

And may that peace come into each of us.

Shanti, shanti, shanti.

Hindu prayer, India
Shanti means
'peace beyond understanding'.

Lord, make me an instrument of your peace.

Where there is hatred, let me sow love.

Where there is injury, pardon.

Where there is discord, vision.

Where there is doubt, faith.

Where there is despair, hope.

Where there is darkness, light.

Where there is sadness, joy.

O divine master,

grant that I may not so much seek

to be consoled as to console,

to be understood as to understand;

to be loved as to love;

for it is in giving that we receive,

it is in pardoning that we are pardoned,

and it is in dying that we are born to eternal life.

Written by Saint Francis of Assisi, who tried to live at peace
with the whole of creation, including the birds and animals.
Italy

*An important step to peace is forgiveness. Once we have forgiven
each other, we no longer have a reason to fight. This prayer finds
reasons to forgive, even when people have done terrible things to us.*

O Lord,

remember not only the men and women of goodwill,

but also those of ill will.

But do not only remember the suffering they have inflicted on us,

remember the fruits we bore thanks to this suffering,

our comradeship, our loyalty, our humility,

the courage, the generosity,

the greatness of heart which has grown out of all this.

And when they come to judgement

let all the fruits which we have borne

be their forgiveness. Amen. Amen. Amen.

Found beside the body of a Jewish child
in a German concentration camp, 1945

When we hear the news, sometimes the bad things in the world seem stronger than the good. These prayers remind us that good can still triumph over bad.

Goodness is stronger than evil,

love is stronger than hate,

light is stronger than darkness;

victory is ours through him who loves us.

Written by Archbishop Desmond Tutu, who helped to bring peace to South Africa in the 1990s

Lead us from death to life,
from falsehood to truth.
Lead us from despair to hope,
from fear to trust.
Lead us from hate to love,
from war to peace.
Let peace fill our hearts, our world, our universe –
peace, peace, peace.

Written by Satish Kumar, a Jain monk. Jains believe that
we should never harm any living being, even the smallest fly.
India

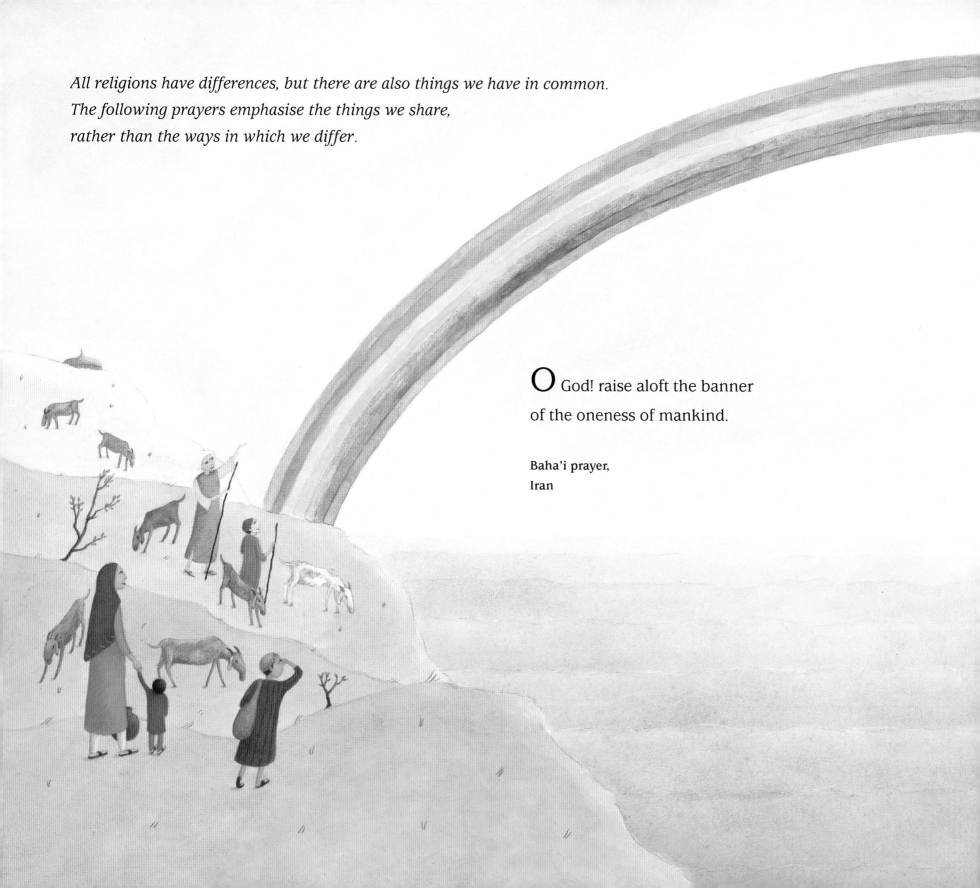

All religions have differences, but there are also things we have in common.
The following prayers emphasise the things we share,
rather than the ways in which we differ.

O God! raise aloft the banner
of the oneness of mankind.

Baha'i prayer,
Iran

Recognise all people as one.

Written by Guru Gobind Singh, Tenth Guru of Sikhism, India

*Conflict is frightening, whether it is in a war or in
our own homes and families. These two prayers
ask God to watch over us.*

Circle me, Lord.
Keep protection near
and danger afar.

Circle me, Lord.
Keep hope within.
Keep doubt without.

Circle me, Lord.
Keep light near
and darkness afar.

Circle me, Lord.
Keep peace within.
Keep evil out.

Lindisfarne Christian Community,
England

God to enfold me,
God to surround me,
God in my speaking,
God in my thinking.

God in my sleeping,
God in my waking,
God in my watching,
God in my hoping.

God in my life,
God in my lips,
God in my soul,
God in my heart.

God in my sufficing,
God in my slumber,
God in mine ever-living soul,
God in my eternity.

Traditional Celtic prayer,
United Kingdom

Let there be peace on Earth and let it begin with me.

Let there be peace on Earth, the peace that was meant to be!

With God our creator, family all are we;

Let us walk with each other in perfect harmony.

Let peace begin with me. Let this be the moment now.

With every step I take, let this be my solemn vow;

To take each moment and live each moment in peace eternally!

Let there be peace on Earth and let it begin with me!

Written by Sy Miller and Jill Jackson,
North America